Complete Internet Privacy

The Quickest Guide to Being Anonymous Online

By Craig Cox

Disclaimer

The following book is provided to the reader "As Is" and is for informational purposes only. The author shall not be liable for any loss or damage caused or allegedly caused by any information contained herein. The author is not responsible for the use of the information in this book by anyone for legal or illegal reasons.

All trademarks mentioned in this book are the property of their respective owners. The author does not claim any ownership over them and has no intention of infringement of any trademark. All trademarks are used in order to help the reader in using the trademarked service and benefit the owner of the trademark by providing help to their users.

ISBN-13: 978-1492702665

ISBN-10: 1492702668

CONTENTS

Introduction

We are being watched. The internet is not private. It was never meant to be. After hearing so many news stories about information being secretly gathered online, people around the world have started to wonder who is watching them online. The smart ones have gone one step further and are now actively seeking a way to protect themselves and their families. Lucky for you, you're one of those people. This guide will give you all the information you need.

There are many different reasons people may want to protect themselves by being anonymous online. While it is true that some people seek online anonymity for illegal purposes, most people just want the security and freedom that comes with privacy.

Remember, the internet was not made to be anonymous. Every connection between users and web pages requires a connection that shares information. It takes a little time and work to be anonymous and protect yourself from being spied on.

There are many different levels of privacy. More privacy means more time spent on ensuring you are anonymous. Sometimes you want to make sure no one in the world knows what you are doing. Other times you just want to make sure other people who use your computer won't see your history. The techniques in this book are arranged from lowest to highest level of security. You can decide what level of privacy is right for you depending on what your needs are.

Keep in mind that all of the information provided in this book is meant to be used only by law-abiding citizens to ensure their privacy and protect them against unreasonable searches. If you break the law, searching your online activities is no longer unreasonable. DO NOT participate in any illegal activities on the internet. You can and will be discovered sooner or later. The right to privacy is not a right to piracy.

Be safe out there.

Quick, Low Level Security: Google Incognito

If you are only worried about your browser history, search history, or cookies being left on your local machine, the fastest way to protect yourself is to use Google Chrome's Incognito window. This will not protect you from any outside sources spying on your activities, but it is an easy way to not leave traces on a local machine. The best part is that it does not affect the history, cookies, or anything else that was already on the computer. This is useful for quickly doing something on another person's computer. You can use an Incognito window to log in to all of your accounts without saving your information on the computer. The computer will look like you were never on it. Nothing will be changed.

Just make sure to remember that Google Incognito is only a quick way to keep your tracks off the machine you are currently using. It does not protect you from being spied on by outside people or entities.

To use this tool, make sure the computer you are on has Google Chrome installed. It can be downloaded here: **https://www.google.com/intl/en/chrome/browser/**. When the browser is opened, simply use the keyboard command Ctrl+Shift+N to open a new tab. You can open an Incognito window by opening the settings on the right side of the address bar. You will know you are in Incognito mode when this icon is on the top-left corner of the screen:

That logo is meant to make *you* feel like the sneaky, trench coat-wearing figure. Instead, think of it as a reminder that *other* sneaky, trench coat-wearing may still be watching. There is even this message placed in the middle of the screen:

You've gone incognito. Pages you view in this window won't appear in your browser history or search history, and they won't leave other traces, like cookies, on your computer after you close **all** open incognito windows. Any files you download or bookmarks you create will be preserved, however.

Going incognito doesn't affect the behavior of other people, servers, or software. Be wary of:

- Websites that collect or share information about you
- Internet service providers or employers that track the pages you visit
- Malicious software that tracks your keystrokes in exchange for free smileys
- Surveillance by secret agents
- People standing behind you

Learn more about incognito browsing.

Because Google Chrome does not control how extensions handle your personal data, all extensions have been disabled for incognito windows. You can reenable them individually in the extensions manager.

It explicitly states that the actions of others, including secret agents, are not affected by using Incognito. Incognito windows can only be used as a quick way to keep others who use your computer from seeing your tracks.

Let's move on to keeping people *outside* your home from getting into your information.

Internet Settings that Work

The first thing you need to do to start using the internet privately is change some settings on your computer. Here's how to get to these settings:

1. Open the Start Menu on the bottom left of the screen
2. Find and open the Control Panel
3. Open your Internet Options

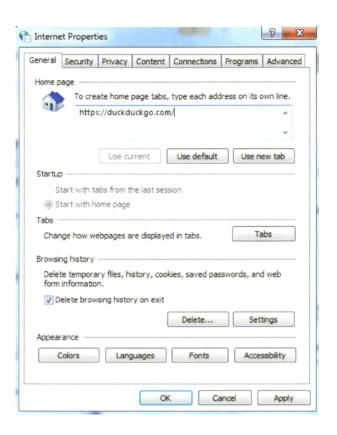

Near the top of this screenshot you can see that my home page is set to **https://duckduckgo.com/**. Duck Duck Go is the leading anonymous search engine on the internet. Unlike most major search engines, they keep your searches private and never collect or share personal data. I highly recommend that you read **http://donttrack.us/** to learn more about why search engines collecting data from you can be a problem. Duck Duck Go's privacy policy is available at **https://duckduckgo.com/privacy** for you to review.

If you like using Incognito windows in Google Chrome because your history isn't stored locally, your computer can be setup to always get rid of your tracks automatically. All you have to do is check the box next to "Delete browsing history on exit".

The next settings to change are under the Privacy tab of the Internet Properties window.

The slider on the left-hand side of this screen controls the permissions for cookies. A cookie is a small file that websites give to users to track them. This is not usually a bad thing. Cookies are not viruses. One purpose of cookies, for example, is to mark a URL as read after you click them by changing the link's color. That can be useful if you frequently visit news sites, forums, or other places with a lot of continually updated information.

It is best to look at the descriptions for each setting on the slider before choosing one. I use the High setting because it provides the benefits of cookies if two strict conditions are met by the website: they must display a compact privacy policy and cannot use cookies that can contact me without my consent. This will work well for most people. However, if you want to be as secure as possible you should choose the option to Block All Cookies. You can always move the slider down a notch if you have any problems with functionality.

The last change to make on this tab is to check the box next to "Never allow websites to request your physical location". This prevents your location from being gathered without your knowledge. Choosing to allow your location to be gathered makes finding things like local news, businesses, and weather more convenient. It can also let just about anyone else pinpoint where you are. Blocking websites from requesting your physical location means you are in control of which websites get information from you and how much they are allowed to know.

Virus Protection

There is no shortage of antivirus programs out there that do a great job protecting you and your computer. AVG, Avast!, Avira, Malwarebytes, Panda and many others all have powerful free versions available on their websites for you to use. Each have their strengths and weaknesses, but you really can't go wrong choosing any of them. The only problem with using the free version of these programs is that they frequently advertise their paid versions.

If you use Windows XP, Vista, or 7, your best option for a powerful, free antivirus without any ads is to use Microsoft Security Essentials (**http://windows.microsoft.com/en-us/windows/security-essentials-download**). It is incredibly easy to use and you even get a lot of features usually reserved for paid versions like real-time protection. It really is surprising that Microsoft didn't include Security Essentials with those operating systems.

Microsoft does include an antivirus in Windows 8, however. It's called Windows Defender and is basically the same as Microsoft Security Essentials is on XP, Vista, and 7. What's confusing is that there use to be a Windows Defender for these older operating systems, but it only handled spyware. Many people disliked the old Defender because of that limitation which is why Microsoft replaced it with Security Essentials. The new Windows 8 version of Defender protects you from spyware, viruses, adware and other malware the same way Security Essentials does for XP, Vista, and 7.

That's confusing, so here is what it all means. If you use Windows XP, Vista, or 7, download Microsoft Security Essentials from the link above. If you use Windows 8, use the provided Windows Defender as your antivirus. Both are the same thing.

Stop Spam Mail

To help keep spam mail from piling up in your inbox you need to have an extra email account. You can sign up for a free account with Google, Yahoo, or any other email provider you like. Use this extra email address anywhere you don't want to give your personal address to. This tip will greatly reduce the amount of spam you have to wade through daily in your usual account. At anytime your extra email address can be abandoned and a new one can be created.

Keep in mind that there are still ways to trace this address back to you. Even though it is not your regular inbox it is still yours.

Creating Secure Passwords

The most regularly overlooked aspect of securely using the internet is having good passwords. You cannot use things like "password", "12345", or your name. Not only are these types of passwords easy for people you know to guess, they are among the first that brute force hacking programs try. These programs automatically go through a long list of common passwords and dictionary words until it finds one that works on your account. Don't let your password be on that list. The more complicated your password is, the less likely it is to be discovered.

The most secure passwords you can use are randomly generated. You can find websites to randomly generate passwords for you, but that means there is a record of your password floating around somewhere on the internet. Not good. Instead, just type at least twelve random numbers, letters in upper and lower case, and symbols until you have something like this: "Ae4$TgP9@h2!".

Sometimes the website will have rules for password creation; one capital letter, one number, one symbol, no symbols. If symbols are allowed, try to use as many as possible. The most important thing is just to have a lot of characters. Twelve is a good number.

Sometimes you want something more memorable for a site you visit frequently. Here's a recipe for a secure, memorable password:

1. Think of something memorable.
2. Misspell the word intentionally to throw off hacking programs that guess dictionary words.
3. Add your favorite number.
4. Throw in a symbol or two.

For example, let's say you have a brother named Hank. You can change the "k" to "q" so the word sounds the same phonetically. Maybe Michael Jordan is your favorite athlete so you choose 23 for the number. Your password could be "Hanq23@!".

Now just keep picturing your brother Hank in a number 23 Michael Jordan Jersey playing basketball. He's dribbling, shooting, dunking, all while wearing that number 23 jersey. For the "@!" part, the question mark almost looks like a baseball bat. Now Hank in his 23 jersey is "at bat" or "@!". It may seem silly, but when you create vivid pictures like this in your mind it becomes very easy to remember things. It's called a mnemonic.

Another tip for passwords is to never use the same one for more than one site. Using the same password everywhere means that a security breach at any site that has your information compromises every account you own. This happens more regularly than you might think. Just look up news about passwords and accounts being hacked to see.

Remembering all your passwords can be very difficult even if you use mnemonics. The absolute most secure way to keep passwords from being taken from your computer is to never store them there. If you aren't worried about anyone in your home finding and using your passwords, the most secure way to store them is on paper. Write all of the websites you use down with your accounts and passwords in a notebook or on a sheet of paper and hide it somewhere near your computer. You could even write all this on the last page of a book. Just make sure that wherever you put this information is secure and it will not be removed from where it belongs.

Another way to save your passwords is to use a cloud-based service like **www.passpack.com** to store them for you. They use TLS/SSL encryption to create a secure connection between you and them. This is the same security banks and online stores use when you connect with them. Many people may not like the idea of a website having access to all your information. That is perfectly fine. Anyone interested in using Passpack should first review their privacy policies at **https://www.passpack.com/en/privacy/** before making a decision. Here's a screenshot for you of the most important part of Passpack's privacy policy:

YOUR PRIVACY

- We try to know as little as possible about you.
- It's okay to use an anonymous email.
- Your info is not sold. traded or disseminated.
- Your email is used for emergencies. notifications and support only.

YOUR RIGHTS

- Change the email associated with your account.
- Delete your account whenever you'd like.
- Ask us what information we have on file for you.
- Request that we delete all traces of you in our systems, including support emails.

Encrypt Your Internet Usage with TLS/SSL

As previously mentioned, TLS/SSL encryption is a great way to establish secure connections to websites. It is available on almost every website that handles any personal information. Unfortunately many sites will send you to the unencrypted version of their site by default. Any site with a URL starting with "http" is not using TLS/SSL encryption. A TLS/SSL encrypted connection is designated by "https" (Hypertext Transfer Protocol Secure) at the beginning of the URL. Look for "https" at the beginning of every webpage to know if it is secure or not. Here's an example:

The URL above uses "https" encryption for security and is also the address to **https://www.eff.org/https-everywhere**. At this website you can download an add-on for Google Chrome and Firefox to connect with TLS/SSL encryption whenever possible. The EFF, or Electronic Frontier Foundation, is an organization created to defend our rights on the internet. In addition to creating this program for anyone to freely use, they have also filed a court case against the NSA over surveillance issues back in 2008.

Block ALL Advertisements and Video

Commercials

Another add-on that will increase your security and also make browsing the web much more enjoyable is Adblock Plus (**https://adblockplus.org/**). It is available for Chrome, Firefox, Opera, Internet Explorer, and even Android phones. Adblock Plus blocks advertisements on websites and commercials on most video sites, including YouTube.

Adblock Plus can also be configured to block malicious domains, remove annoying social media sharing buttons and disable tracking. After installing, you should see this screen:

Adblock Plus has been installed

Adblock Plus will always block annoying ads. Still, we want to encourage websites using plain and unobtrusive advertising. That's why we have established strict guidelines to identify acceptable ads, and allow these out of the box. You can always disable this if you want to block all ads.

Adblock Plus can do more than blocking ads:

 Malware Blocking: Block domains that are known to be infected by malware to make browsing the internet more secure.

 Remove Social Media Buttons: Remove social media integration such as the Facebook Like button that track your browsing habits.

 Disable Tracking: There are hundreds of ad companies tracking your every move, but you can easily disable all tracking to browse privately.

Just click each slider to change them from off to on. If this screen does not show up or you just want to know more about Adblock Plus before installing, visit **https://adblockplus.org/en/features**. You can also visit this page at any time to remove any of these features.

Stop Being Tracked by Google Analytics

Google Analytics is a tool that web developers use to analyze the traffic that visits their sites. This tool gives them access to your IP address and information about you including your location, browser, and operating system. If you would like to opt-out of this program, download the add-on for your browser at **https://tools.google.com/dlpage/gaoptout**. Whenever a website uses Google Analytics, this add-on will tell the tool that your information is off limits and will keep web developers from receiving data from you.

How Proxy Servers Hide Your Identity

A big part of being anonymous and secure on the internet is to keep your IP address from being seen. An IP address is a unique string of digits used to identify every user and every website on the internet. It's like a name tag. You can see what your IP address is at
http://www.whatismyip.com/.

Imagine you're at a party where no one knows each other but everyone has name tags on. Every person you interact with sees your name tag. This is basically how the internet works. When you connect to a website, you are giving them your IP address and receiving theirs. This exchange happens every time you visit any website. The problem is that anyone who wants to spy on you can peek in on this interaction and collect information about you.

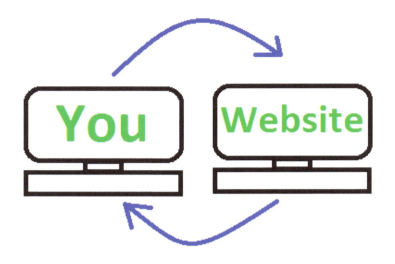

So, back to the party analogy. How could you talk with anyone in the room without others knowing you were involved in those interactions?

Simple. Wear a fake name tag.

You can basically do the same thing online. Instead of wearing a fake name tag you use a proxy service to fool internet snoopers into thinking you are someone other than yourself. These proxy services will lend you a different IP address to use as your name tag while you surf the web. The bad guys will see the proxy's IP address instead of yours. What really makes this process work is that it's not just you with a fake name tag. Many other users are using the same IP. That makes it extremely difficult to figure out exactly who is visiting what site.

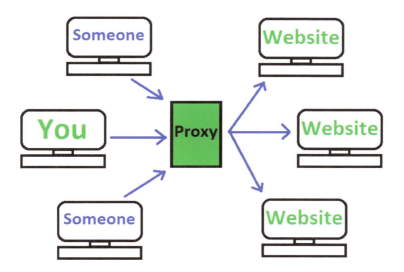

There are a couple different types of proxies that you can use. Each has benefits and issues that should be considered before using one.

Web proxies like **www.hidemyass.com** and other similar sites found on the list at **http://proxy.org/** are very easy to use. They look and act the same as a search engine. The biggest problem with using a web proxy is that they can often be slow or completely offline and are sometimes not entirely secure (read this post about a recent issue with HideMyAss: **http://blog.hidemyass.com/2011/09/23/lulzsec-fiasco/**). Another problem is that they can only be used to visit websites. This means they won't work with any programs outside of your browser, including torrent downloading clients. High school students have used these for years to play games and log onto social media sites that are blocked at school.

If you're looking for something to use with torrents, FTP clients, or any other programs outside of your browser, you need a SOCKS proxy. These can handle all of your online activities. Lists of SOCKS proxy IP's can be found at websites like **http://www.sockslist.net/**. All you have to do is check to make sure it is still working and plug it into your programs settings. The directions for using a proxy will be different for each program, so it is best to do a search on "How to use a proxy with (PROGRAM NAME HERE)" and look for instructions.

Just like web proxies, SOCKS proxies are prone to slow speeds and downtime. The bigger problem is that every time a SOCKS proxy fails you will need to find a new one to replace the old one in all of your program's settings. Depending on how many programs and browsers you use a proxy for, this can take some time.

Web and SOCKS proxies main benefit is that they are both free. If you need something more reliable and even more secure it is best to pay for a Virtual Private Network.

More Encryption with Virtual Private Networks (VPN)

Unlike a proxy which only conceals your IP address, a Virtual Private Network uses powerful encryption (up to 2048-bit) to secure all of your online activity. You do not need to set it up to work with each program individually as you would with a proxy. Every connection is secured automatically after you log on to your VPN's client program. VPN's are also more secure than proxies because your traffic is not sent through a middleman: you are able to interact with the internet directly. The only benefits proxies have over VPNs is that they are usually free and sometimes slightly faster.

There are a lot of great VPNs to choose from. The most important thing to consider when choosing a service is whether or not it logs the activities of its users. There is no point in paying for any VPN that keeps logs. The reason for this is that while VPNs are not required to log their users activity, they are legally obligated to hand over any records they *do* keep to internet service providers and governments when they are asked for. For more information on choosing a VPN service and my latest recommendation for which to use, please visit my website at **completeinternetprivacy.com/vpn/**. Using a good VPN is essential to your internet security and privacy.

The exact instructions for how to install and run your VPN will vary depending on the service you choose. Your provider should give you all the information you need. If you have any trouble installing or running your VPN client simply google "how to use (VPN NAME HERE)" for directions specific to your service.

Ultimate Anonymity

If maximum privacy is your goal, Tor is your answer (**https://www.torproject.org/download/download-easy.html.en**). Tor, short for The Onion Router, is like a proxy on steroids. Instead of sending your traffic through just one proxy, Tor sends it through three random "relays" in its network before finally connecting with the internet. These relays are other computers, just like yours, across the globe.

In addition to all of this, Tor also uses encryption to protect you. Their user manual (available at **https://www.torproject.org/dist/manual/short-user-manual_en.xhtml**) explains that "Tor will anonymize the origin of your traffic, and it will encrypt everything between you and the Tor network. Tor will also encrypt your traffic inside the Tor network, but it cannot encrypt your traffic between the Tor network and its final destination". Because there is no way to encrypt the traffic you send between the last relay and its ultimate destination, there is always the possibility of that relay eavesdropping.

One way you can minimize your risk of this happening is to always use HTTPS. Fortunately, Tor comes preinstalled with the HTTPS Everywhere extension discussed previously in the TLS/SSL section of this book. Be sure to look for "https" at the beginning of every URL you visit to make sure the connection is secure.

EFF, the makers of HTTPS Everywhere, have put together a diagram at https://www.eff.org/pages/tor-and-https explaining what information is available to others when using Tor, HTTPS, both together, or no protection at all. Take a look at it to familiarize yourself with what exactly these services can do for you.

One thing that you may notice from the diagram linked to above is that there is no way of hiding when Tor is being used. This is the one downside of the service. Although Tor is used worldwide by many people completely legally, there is a large number of people who use Tor to hide their illegal activities. There is an entire area of the internet only accessible through Tor containing many different types of illegal material like drug trafficking

If you choose to use Tor, do so knowing that it may draw attention because of what some other people use it for. Even though the majority of Tor users are probably using it legally, it is important to always be mindful of who you may be associated with. Just be careful and only use Tor legally.

If you still want to use Tor you can download it from **https://www.torproject.org/download/download-easy.html.en**. Right-click and extract the files somewhere you will easily remember, like the desktop. Click the "Start Tor Browser" button in the extracted folder to load the Vidalia Control Panel and a browser window with this message:

The Tor browser, based on Firefox, will behave like any other browser. The Vidalia Control Panel is where all your settings for Tor and your status on the network is located.

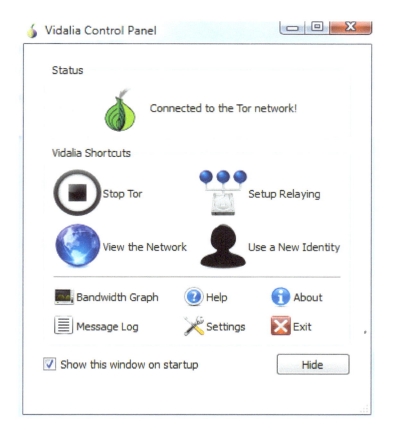

The "Use a New Identity" button is used to change your IP address. Nothing else on the Vidalia Control Panel is necessary for most users. All the default settings will work fine.

Even though you are almost completely anonymous using Tor, there is always the possibility of your activities being monitored when you are online if someone suspects that you are breaking the law. There has been news recently of the NSA and other law enforcement agencies gaining access to Tor users' identities and prosecuting individuals for illegal activities. As stated in the introduction to this book, all of the information provided in this book is meant to be used only by law-abiding citizens to ensure their privacy and protect them against unreasonable searches. If you break the law, searching your online activities is no longer unreasonable. DO NOT participate in any illegal activities on the internet.

Use Someone Else's Computer Without Them

Knowing

So far all of the information in this book has been aimed at helping you use your own PC privately and securely. Most of the time this is enough. Sometimes, however, you need to use another computer anonymously. It would take too long to get everything set up like you have on your computer and it would be pretty obvious to others that you have changed settings, downloaded programs, and actively made an effort to be anonymous. For a more discrete way to surf the web outside your home, there is Tails.

Tails, The Amnesic Incognito Live System, is a combination of Linux and Tor designed to be mobile. It can be loaded onto a USB drive or burned to a DVD and carried with you anywhere. No traces of your internet activities or use of this program are left on the computer or on the web.

The most secure way to use Tails is to burn it to a DVD-R. Although it can be run on USB drives and DVD-RW discs, both of these options are rewriteable and therefore have a security flaw. Another person could possibly load tracking software to either and follow your activities. A plain DVD-R on the other hand can only be written to once. There is no way to put any data on the disk after you burn it the first time.

To get started, you first need to download the ISO image from **https://tails.boum.org/download/index.en.html**. You'll see the following ISO download link under step 2:

An ISO image is kind of like a ZIP file meant for burning disks: it contains a lot of data in a single file meant to be easily transported. This ISO image is what you will be burning to your disk later.

Before you do that, the ISO file needs to be verified. The Tails website has all the instructions at **https://tails.boum.org/download/index.en.html#verify**. For windows users, select "Using other operating systems" and follow the steps. The verification steps may seem superfluous, but it is absolutely necessary to ensure your file has not been compromised. There is no point in using a program meant for security if it has been altered by someone.

After your copy of Tails is verified, you are ready to burn your disk. Windows 7 and Windows 8 have programs that can do this. When you right-click the ISO file you should see an option to burn the disc image. These is a Windows 7 ISO guide at **http://windows.microsoft.com/en-us/windows7/burn-a-cd-or-dvd-from-an-iso-file** and a Windows 8 ISO guide at **http://theunlockr.com/2013/04/25/how-to-burn-iso-files-in-windows-8/** if you need more information.

If you use another version of Windows you will need to download an ISO image mounting program. ImgBurn, available for download at **http://www.imgburn.com/index.php?act=downloadhttp://www.imgburn.com/index.php?act=download**, is free and very easy to use. The only problem is that their download page has ads that try to trick you into thinking they are what you need to click, like this:

If you installed Adblock Plus you shouldn't see any of these ads. The real download links are the mirror sites listed on the middle of the page, like this:

Before you download:
Click here to run a free scan for outdated drivers

Mirror 1 - Provided by Digital Digest   (Currently hosting v2.5.8.0)
Mirror 2 - Provided by BetaNews   (Currently hosting v2.5.8.0)
Mirror 3 - Provided by Softpedia   (Currently hosting v2.5.8.0)
Mirror 4 - Provided by Free-Codecs.com   (Currently hosting v2.5.8.0)
Mirror 5 - Provided by TechSpot   (Currently hosting v2.5.8.0)
Mirror 6 - Provided by MajorGeeks   (Currently hosting v2.5.8.0)
Mirror 7 - Provided by ImgBurn   (Currently hosting v2.5.8.0)

CRC32: 00E8E0B2
MD5: 9685E1B00B7D1B31EDE436BD9B12BE39
SHA-1: 5CA96A0C243390C378DEE1A629684EA261E2CFC4

Any mirror will work, but it's always best to download from the source

If you click one and it doesn't work, just try another. After ImgBurn is installed and loaded, you will see this screen:

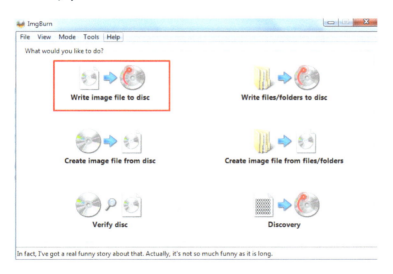

Click "Write image file to disc" and this screen will appear:

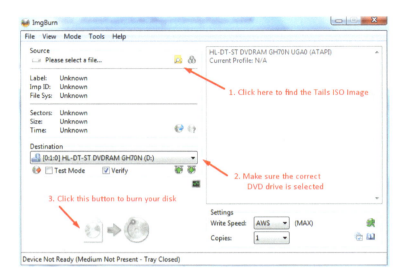

Now that you've burned your Tails disk, insert it into the computer's drive and restart the computer. Tails should automatically load a welcome screen and ask you to select your language. Congratulations!

If Tails does not load you will have to change a setting in the BIOS to make the computer boot from the DVD drive first. This is not hard to do and doing it correctly should not cause any problems on the computer, but it is possible to mess up other settings in the BIOS that will compromise the computers stability. Please do not alter any settings that you are unfamiliar with. Anything you change is your responsibility.

When the computer first loads you should see a message telling you what key to press to enter the BIOS settings or setup utilities. Usually this is the Delete key but could also be Esc, any of the F buttons at the top of your keyboard, or a combination of other keys. Use whatever key or keys this screen instructs you to.

The BIOS screen is usually blue or gray and will only have text. Somewhere on this screen should be an option to change the computers boot sequence. What you need to do is change the boot sequence so the optical drive is at the top of the list and the hard drive is somewhere below it. This change will make the computer look for an operating system on a disk (Tails) before it loads the regular OS from the hard drive.

Just like when using Tor, there is always the possibility when using Tails of your activities being monitored if someone suspects that you are breaking the law. As mentioned previously, all of the information provided in this book is meant to be used only by law-abiding citizens to ensure their privacy and protect them against unreasonable searches. If you break the law, searching your online activities is no longer unreasonable. DO NOT participate in any illegal activities.

www.ingramcontent.com/pod-product-compliance
Lightning Source LLC
Chambersburg PA
CBHW041146050326
40689CB00001B/511